Who are you? What makes you, YOU? There are so many things that can help shape who you are and how you see the world. Some of those things might be people, places, foods, maybe even objects in your house... like a rug.

We live in a world that is exceptionally diverse, but often it is easier to blend in than it is to stand out. In "It's Just a Rug", three friends learn what helps make each of them unique and special, and how their different heritages play a role in that. In her children's book debut, Jodi-Tatiana Charles partners with artist Diana Lisanto to encourage children to be curious about the family that came before them, and to celebrate the beautiful things that their cultures can impart on them as individuals.

"It's Just a Rug" is a story that reminds us that getting to know ourselves, and to celebrate our differences, is its own important and exciting adventure! The author invites you, readers of all ages, to become curious about your own heritage, and to start weaving your own rug with the stories of your life.

It's Just a Rug

Written by
Jodi-Tatiana Charles

Illustrated by
Diana Lisanto

This is a work of fiction. Names, characters, places and incidents either are the product of the author's imagination or are used fictitiously. Any resemblance to actual persons, living or dead, events, or locales is entirely coincidental.

All rights reserved. Published in the United States by Necto Inc., Massachusetts

Text © 2017 by Jodi-Tatiana Charles
Illustrations © 2017 by Diana Lisanto
Jacket art © 2017 by Diana Lisanto

Edited by Emily Dahlgaard Thor

Library of Congress Control Number: 2018901152
hardcover - ISBN-13: 978-0-9995458-0-5
paperback - ISBN-13: 978-0-9995458-9-8
ebook - ISBN-13: 978-0-9995458-4-3

Special thank you to Phoebe Juves, Christopher Denaro, Marjan Tabari, Hearns Charles, Toni Pruitt, Sarah Cabe, Hervé Bruce, Christine Loeber, Jose Rolon, Lisa Willis, Maryse Prophete, Alvine Stallworth, Nick Naraghi, Alison Underhill, Kathy Wilder, Merry Chin, Katy O'Neil, Michelle McCarthy, Erin Trabucco, Wrigley Blaney, Loreen "Sam" Watts, Kathy Snyder, John Snyder, Ali Nigro, Luz Arregoces, Joselin Mane, Patrick Swidler, Veronica N. Chapman, Cianna Winnick, Diana Vertus, Keith Spiro, Chara Itoka, Colette Greenstein, and all our diverse communities.

For my beautiful daddy Raymond and my grandmother Momie Za, you are both missed so very much. Thanks to my mom Jacqueline, family and friends for always supporting me.

~ Jodi-Tatiana

For my mom Cinda, who made sure we never ate pasta sauce out of a jar. The Italian traditions you pass to me don't always make sense, but they're all part of what makes up our colorful family "rug".

~ Diana

Dalir, Zazoo, and Bertie, are excited to be getting out of school! Today is an early release day.

What a surprise! Dalir's mom Sara brought Persia, his new puppy.

Normally after school, Dalir's mom would bring them straight to soccer practice, but today is special; they are going to visit Dalir's Maman Bozorg Homa. Maman Bozorg means grandmother.

Before they knew it, they had arrived.
Dalir, Zazoo, Bertie, and Persia run to greet Homa.

Homa greets everyone just outside the door.

"Hi, Maman Bozorg Homa," "Hi Homa," "Hi Homa," they all yell one at a time.

Homa gives everyone a hug and a cookie as they enter the house.

The children's giggles and Persia's barking draw Sara to the living room.

"Dalir, you know the rules," says his mother in a stern voice, "no playing on Maman Bozorg Homa's rug."

Dalir looks up, knowing he is in a bit of trouble. Cautiously he says, "But Mom, it's just a rug."

The others chime in, "Yeah, it's just a rug!"

Sara looks at the children as Persia pulls at a piece of the rug. She is about to say something when Homa calls everyone in for lunch,
"Lunch is ready!"

As they sit at the table, Dalir's grandmother passes around plates of Kabab Koobideh with Persian Steamed Rice and Sangak.

His mother serves small bowls of something like rice pudding, Shir Berenj with strawberries.

These are traditional foods from the family's homeland of Persia.

As he reaches for his plate, Dalir asks Maman Bozorg, "Why can't we play on the rug?"

In a soft voice Homa replies, "The rug is part of our story. It reminds us of our homeland and its foods, special occasions, and family members that are no longer with us," she paused, "What do you remember about the rug?"

Zazoo gets up to go view the rug,
but Homa stops her and says with a smile,
"What do you remember WITHOUT going to look at it?"

Bertie clears his voice after swallowing his food, "I remember the birds." Zazoo replies quickly, "I didn't see any birds!"

"There were actually seven birds, I counted them," he replies, while finishing his last bite, never looking up.

"You are correct Bertie, they are called the Homa Birds," Homa assures him.
Dalir replies in excitement, "Like your name, Homa!"

"Exactly. What else do you notice about the rug?" Homa asks.

Dalir's mother cleans up as his grandmother leads everyone into the living room.

"There are bright colors," Zazoo bursts. "And look at the fruits!"

Homa sits in a big green chair, with Persia on her lap. The children gather on the floor.

Homa explains more, "My Baba-Bozorg Ervin, my grandfather, was a master dye maker. He used fruits, flowers, snails, and even insects from his region."

Together they look towards the rug and say, "Ewwwww bugs," and laugh.

Bertie asks, "Did he make this rug too?"

"Baba-Bozorg Ervin mixed the colors, but it was his wife Donya that made the rug," Homa replies, "They were a very good team! They combined stories from their childhood memories, and Donya used her weaving skills to tell those stories with this rug."

They look at the rug closely.

Homa continues, "The colors, wool, design, and images woven together inside this very old rug are part of our story of being Persian."
They exclaim together, "Wowww!"

Homa asks Zazoo and Bertie, "Can you share some stories from your families?"

They look at each other and shrug their shoulders.

The three go home for the evening and find themselves curious to learn as much as they can about their families.

Their questions come fast and seem endless.

They ask about countries, foods, traditions, clothes, music, and more.

The next morning, Zazoo makes traditional Haitian pâté – which are meat or fish-filled pastries – as her parents watch over her. They share stories with her from their homeland, a country on the island of Hispaniola.

Bertie's father shows him photos of relatives and uses maps and globes to point out some of the locations his family came from in Italy.

Dalir returns to Homa's house and runs around her living room, placing objects on her lap, waiting for the next story she can share.

From another room his mother says, "Dalir, let Homa rest; it's time to get ready for your soccer game."

Now it's almost game time.
Families are gathered on the sideline while some children are practicing on the field.

Zazoo sings to herself, swinging her head from side to side, "Jouu-mou jouu-mou jouu-mou, Zazoo loves jouu-mou!"

"What's joy mooo?" asks Dalir.

"Nooo, Jouuu-Mou!" Zazoo exclaims with a lot of energy and happiness. "Joumou is a soup, a special soup that Haitian families make to celebrate their Independence Day, and New Years Day, too."

"Did your Mom and Dad tell you that?" asks Bertie. "Yup, and so much more!" she says. Then she asks, "What did your dad tell you?"

"He told me that our family is from a few different parts of Italy. My Dad's family is from Sicily. There is a small group of people with red hair like me that live there. They are called the Normans."

Zazoo and Dalir respond together, "Coooool!!!"

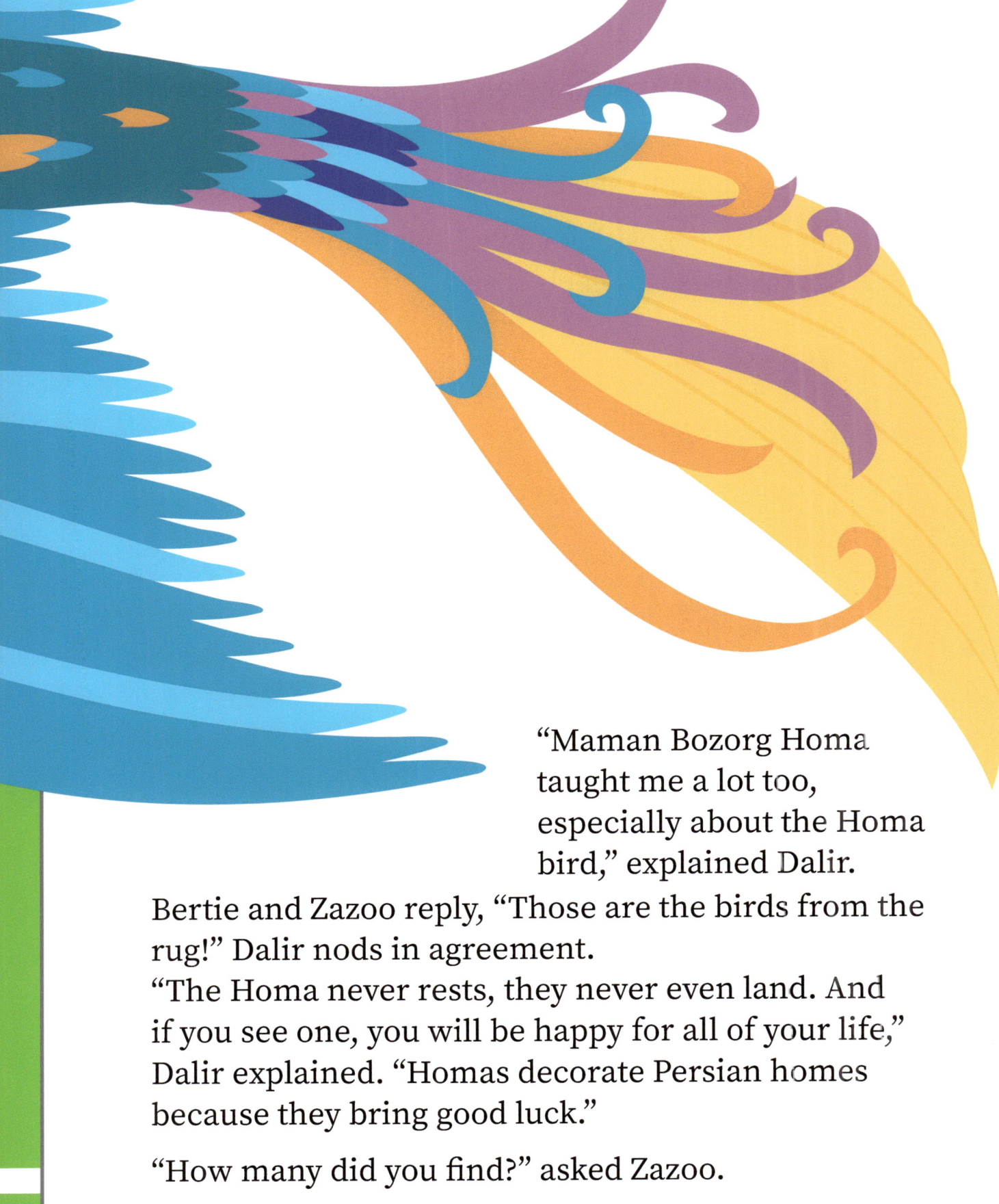

"Maman Bozorg Homa taught me a lot too, especially about the Homa bird," explained Dalir.

Bertie and Zazoo reply, "Those are the birds from the rug!" Dalir nods in agreement.

"The Homa never rests, they never even land. And if you see one, you will be happy for all of your life," Dalir explained. "Homas decorate Persian homes because they bring good luck."

"How many did you find?" asked Zazoo.

Dalir expels a deep breath, "I'm still counting; they are everyyywhere!"

They continue to share their discoveries with one another, with smiles and laughter, when they are interrupted by the sound of a whistle.

The game is about to start.

They run to their positions delighted, knowing a bit more about themselves and each other.

The End

How many homa birds did YOU find?

 JODI-TATIANA CHARLES is a first generation American born to loving Haitian parents and a self-made grandmother. Her strong family roots have instilled in her a pride in her family's culture and heritage, and she wants to share that celebration of diversity with her readers. She is always curious to seek out new and adventurous ways to learn and to embrace others for their differences and unique qualities. She is an avid global traveler and dedicates her time to children, the elderly, and cancer causes, through road races, mentoring, and volunteering. Following in her grandmother's footsteps, she has crafted a career of educating entrepreneurs, non-profit organizations, and small-business professionals on the importance of growing and marketing their unique brands. She lives in her beloved community of Marblehead, Massachusetts.

 DIANA LISANTO started her illustrating ways as a kid, drawing characters on her desk in elementary school. She continued to draw and create into adulthood, graduating from Syracuse University with a BFA in Illustration. She now lives in Boston, MA as a graphic designer and freelance illustrator. Her main goal whenever she illustrates is humor. If she doesn't find herself laughing while working, she knows something isn't right. Her work may be geared towards children, but she believes it can be appreciated and loved by all ages.

CPSIA information can be obtained
at www.ICGtesting.com
Printed in the USA
BVHW02n0221050418
512556BV00009B/24/P